Copyright 2023 Forthma

All rights reserved. No part of this publication may be reproduced, distributed, or transmitted in any form or by any means, including photocopying, recording, or other electronic or mechanical methods, without the prior written permission of the publisher, except in the case of brief quotations embodied in critical reviews and certain other noncommercial uses permitted by copyright law.

Rome Travel Guide

Contents

Chapter 1

Introduction to Rome: History, Culture, and Attractions

- Overview of Rome's history and cultural significance
- Introduction to major attractions, such as the Colosseum, Pantheon, and Vatican City

Chapter 2

Planning Your Trip to Rome

- When to visit Rome and how to get there
- Accommodation options and how to book them
- Budgeting and money-saving tips for Rome

Chapter 3

Exploring Ancient Rome

- Visiting the Colosseum and Roman Forum

- Exploring the Palatine Hill and Circus Maximus
- Learning about the history and architecture of ancient Rome

Chapter 4

Discovering the Art and Architecture of Rome

- Exploring the Vatican Museums and St. Peter's Basilica
- Discovering the Renaissance art and architecture of Rome

Chapter 5

Rome's Neighborhoods and Local Culture

- Exploring Trastevere, the Jewish Ghetto, and other unique neighborhoods
- Sampling local Roman cuisine and wine
- Experiencing Rome's nightlife and entertainment scene

Chapter 6

Practical Information for Visiting Rome

Essential travel tips for visiting Rome, such as transportation and safety
- Common Italian phrases and customs to know
- Practical information on visas, health, and insurance for Rome travel

Chapter 1

Introduction to Rome: History, Culture, and Attractions

Overview of Rome's history and cultural significance

Rome is one of the world's most iconic cities, known for its rich history, stunning architecture, and cultural significance. Founded in 753 BC, Rome is one of the oldest continuously inhabited cities in the world, with a history that spans more than two and a half millennia. Over the centuries, Rome has been home to some of the world's most famous emperors, artists, and thinkers, and its influence on Western civilization is immeasurable.

The history of Rome can be divided into several distinct periods. The earliest of these is the Roman Kingdom, which lasted from 753 to 509 BC. During this time, Rome was ruled by a series of kings, the most famous of whom was Romulus, the city's legendary founder. The Roman Republic followed, lasting from 509 to 27 BC, during which Rome was ruled by a senate and a series of elected officials. The Roman Republic was characterized by its expansionism and military prowess, with Rome conquering much of Italy and parts of Greece and Spain.

In 27 BC, Rome became an empire, with Augustus Caesar as its first emperor. The Roman Empire lasted for more than four centuries, during which Rome became the dominant power in the Mediterranean world. The empire was characterized by its military might, engineering feats, and cultural achievements. Rome's most famous landmarks, such as the Colosseum and the Pantheon, were built during this time, as were many of the city's aqueducts and roads.

After the fall of the Western Roman Empire in 476 AD, Rome went through a period of decline and upheaval. The city was sacked by several barbarian tribes, and its population declined significantly. However, Rome remained an important center of Christianity, with the Vatican City becoming the seat of the Catholic Church in the 8th century.

During the Renaissance, Rome experienced a cultural and artistic revival, with many of its most famous landmarks being restored and rebuilt. Artists such as Michelangelo, Raphael, and Bernini all worked in Rome during this time, creating some of the world's most iconic works of art.

In the 19th century, Rome became the capital of a united Italy, and the city underwent a period of modernization and expansion. Today, Rome is one of the world's most popular tourist destinations, with millions of visitors flocking to the city each year to see its ancient ruins, stunning architecture, and vibrant culture.

Rome's cultural significance can be seen in many aspects of modern life. The city has influenced everything from politics to religion to art, and its legacy can be felt around the world. Rome's contribution to Western civilization includes its language, laws, and social institutions, as well as its art, architecture, and philosophy. The city's impact on the world is immeasurable, and its importance in history cannot be overstated.

In conclusion, Rome's historyand cultural significance is vast and complex, spanning thousands of years and encompassing a multitude of different civilizations, empires, and cultural movements. From the ancient Romans to the Renaissance artists to the modern-day city dwellers, Rome has been a hub of creativity, innovation, and intellectual thought.

One of the most notable features of Rome's cultural significance is its role in shaping Western civilization. From the earliest days of the Roman Republic to the height of the Roman Empire, Rome's political, legal, and social institutions set the standard for much of the Western world. The concept of democracy, the rule of law, and the idea of citizenship all have roots in ancient Rome. The Latin language, which was spoken by the ancient Romans, has also had a profound impact on the development of modern European languages.

Rome's impact on the world of art and architecture is equally significant. From the ancient Roman structures such as the Colosseum and the Pantheon to the Renaissance masterpieces of Michelangelo and Raphael, Rome's architecture and art have influenced artists and architects for centuries. Rome has also been a center of Christian art and culture, with the Vatican City housing some of the most famous religious works of art in the world, such as Michelangelo's Sistine Chapel ceiling and Bernini's St. Peter's Square.

Rome's cultural significance is not limited to its art and architecture, however. The city has also played a pivotal role in the development of religion, philosophy, and science. The Catholic Church, which is based in Rome, has been a major force in shaping Western religion, and Rome has been a center of philosophical and scientific thought for centuries.

In addition to its historical and cultural significance, Rome is also a vibrant and modern city with a rich cultural life. Its streets are filled with museums, galleries, and cultural events, and its people are proud of their city's heritage and traditions. From the lively street markets to the famous Italian cuisine, Rome's culture is alive and well, and visitors can experience it firsthand by exploring the city's neighborhoods, shops, and restaurants.

Introduction to major attractions, such as the Colosseum, Pantheon, and Vatican City

Rome is home to some of the most iconic landmarks and attractions in the world, drawing millions of visitors each year from all corners of the globe. From ancient ruins to Renaissance masterpieces to the seat of the Catholic Church, the city offers a rich and diverse cultural experience that is unmatched anywhere else. In this article, we will explore some of the major attractions in Rome, including the Colosseum, Pantheon, and Vatican City.

The Colosseum

    The Colosseum is perhaps Rome's most famous landmark, and is considered one of the Seven Wonders of the World. Built nearly 2,000 years ago, this massive amphitheater was used for gladiatorial contests, public spectacles, and other events. Despite its age and the damage it has sustained over the centuries, the Colosseum remains an impressive sight, and visitors can tour its interior and learn about the fascinating history of this ancient arena.

The Pantheon

is another ancient Roman structure that is a must-see for visitors to Rome. Originally built as a temple to all the gods, this architectural masterpiece features a

massive domed ceiling, intricate marble flooring, and a stunning oculus at its center that lets in natural light. The Pantheon has been used as a church since the 7th century, and is now a popular tourist

attraction that showcases the enduring beauty and engineering prowess of ancient Rome.

The Vatican City is a city-state located within Rome, and is home to the headquarters of the Catholic Church. This tiny country boasts a wealth of art and history, including the world-famous Sistine Chapel, which features Michelangelo's stunning ceiling frescoes. Visitors can also explore the Vatican Museums, which house a vast collection of artwork and historical artifacts, and visit St. Peter's Basilica, one of the Biggest and Largest churches in the world.

Other notable attractions in Rome include the Trevi Fountain, the Spanish Steps, and the Roman Forum, among many others. Whether you're interested in ancient history, religious landmarks, or modern Italian culture, Rome offers a wealth of sights and experiences that are sure to leave you enchanted and inspired.

Detailed Guide on exploring major attractions, such as the Colosseum, Pantheon, and Vatican City in rome

Rome, the Eternal City, is home to some of the world's most famous landmarks and attractions, drawing millions of visitors each year. From ancient ruins to Renaissance masterpieces to the center of the Catholic Church, the city offers a rich and diverse cultural experience that is unmatched anywhere else. In this guide, we will explore some of the major attractions in Rome, including the Colosseum, Pantheon, and Vatican City, and provide relevant information to help you plan your visit.

The Colosseum

The Colosseum, also known as the Flavian Amphitheatre, is perhaps Rome's most famous landmark. Built nearly 2,000 years ago, this massive amphitheater was used for gladiatorial contests, public spectacles, and other events. Despite its age and the damage it has sustained over the centuries, the Colosseum remains an impressive sight, and visitors can tour its interior and learn about the fascinating history of this ancient arena.

Visiting the Colosseum: The Colosseum is located in the heart of Rome, and can be reached by metro, bus, or taxi. The site is open every day except for Christmas Day and New Year's Day, and admission tickets can be purchased online in advance or at the ticket office on site. Visitors should expect long lines and crowds, especially during peak tourist season, and may want to consider a guided tour to avoid the crowds and learn more about the history of this iconic landmark.

The Pantheon

The Pantheon is another ancient Roman structure that is a must-see for visitors to Rome. Originally built as a temple to all the gods, this architectural masterpiece features a massive domed ceiling, intricate marble flooring, and a stunning oculus at its center that lets in natural light. The Pantheon has been used as a church since the 7th century, and is now a popular tourist attraction that showcases the enduring beauty and engineering prowess of ancient Rome.

Visiting the Pantheon: The Pantheon is located in the heart of Rome, and can be reached by metro, bus, or taxi. The site is free to enter and is open every day, although hours may vary on holidays. Visitors should be aware that the Pantheon is an active church and may be closed for services, and should also be prepared for large crowds, especially during peak tourist season.

Vatican City

Vatican City is a city-state located within Rome and is home to the headquarters of the Catholic Church. This tiny country boasts a wealth of art and history, including the world-famous Sistine Chapel, which features Michelangelo's stunning ceiling frescoes. Visitors can also explore the Vatican Museums, which house a vast collection of artwork and historical artifacts.

Visiting Vatican City: Vatican City is located just across the Tiber River from central Rome and can be reached by metro, bus, or taxi. The site is open every day except for Sundays and religious holidays, and admission tickets can be purchased online in advance or at the ticket office on site. Visitors should be aware that the dress code is strict, with no shorts, bare shoulders, or short skirts allowed, and that security can be tight, with long lines and bag checks. Visitors may also want to consider a guided tour to help navigate the complex and learn more about the art and history of this iconic site.

The Colosseum, also known as the Flavian Amphitheatre, is one of the most iconic landmarks in Rome, Italy. If you're planning to visit the Colosseum, here's a guide to help you make the most of your trip.

Address and Location:

The Colosseum is located at Piazza del Colosseo, 1, 00184 Rome, Italy. It is situated in the heart of Rome, just east of the Roman Forum and Palatine Hill. The site is easily accessible by public transportation, including metro, bus, and taxi.

Opening Hours:

The Colosseum is open every day of the week except for Christmas Day and New Year's Day. The site opens at 8:30 am and closes one hour before sunset, which varies depending on the season. Visitors are advised to arrive early in the morning or later in the afternoon to avoid the crowds.

Admission Tickets:

To enter the Colosseum, visitors must purchase an admission ticket. There are many options for purchasing tickets:

- Online: You can purchase tickets online through the official website of the Colosseum, which is recommended to avoid long lines.
- Ticket Office: Tickets can also be purchased at the ticket office on site, but be prepared for long lines, especially during peak tourist season.
- Roma Pass: If you're planning to visit other attractions in Rome, you may want to consider purchasing a Roma Pass, which includes admission to the Colosseum and other sites, as well as free public transportation.

Guided Tours:

To enhance your experience, you may want to consider a guided tour of the Colosseum. Guided tours offer insight into the history and architecture of the site, and also allow you to skip the long lines for admission. There are several options for guided tours, including private tours, small group tours, and audio-guided tours.

What to See and Do:

The Colosseum is a massive amphitheater that was used for gladiatorial contests, public spectacles, and other events. Visitors can explore the interior of the Colosseum, which includes the arena floor, the underground chambers where gladiators and animals were kept, and the upper levels where spectators sat. Along with exploring the Colosseum, visitors can also visit the nearby Roman Forum and Palatine Hill, which offer additional insight into ancient Roman history.

Tips for Visitors:

- Wear comfortable shoes: The Colosseum is a large site, and visitors can expect to do a lot of walking. Wear comfortable shoes to ensure that you can explore the site comfortably.
- Stay hydrated: The summer months in Rome can be hot and humid, so be sure to bring water and stay hydrated throughout your visit.
- Dress appropriately: The Colosseum is a historical site, and visitors are expected to dress appropriately. Avoid wearing revealing clothing, and be prepared to cover your shoulders and knees.
- Be prepared for crowds: The Colosseum is a popular attraction, and visitors should be prepared for long lines and crowds, especially during peak tourist season.
- Follow the rules: The Colosseum is a historical site, and visitors are expected to follow the rules and regulations of the site. Do not touch or climb on any of the structures, and respect the site's historical significance.

In conclusion, the Colosseum is a must-see attraction for visitors to Rome. With its rich history and stunning architecture, it offers a glimpse into ancient Rome and the spectacles that took place there. By following these tips and planning your visit in advance, you can make the most of your trip to this iconic landmark.

The official website of the Colosseum is http://www.coopculture.it/en/colosseo-e-shop.cfm

Here is how to Locate The Colosseum using google map

To locate the Colosseum using Google Maps, follow these steps:

1. Open Google Maps on your device or computer.
2. Type "Colosseum" into the search bar at the top of the screen.

3. The map will show the location of the Colosseum in Rome, Italy, with a red marker.
4. You can zoom in or out on the map to see the surrounding area and nearby attractions.
5. To get directions to the Colosseum from your current location or another destination, click on the blue "Directions" button and enter your starting point or destination.

From there, you can use the map to navigate to the Colosseum and explore the surrounding area.

The Pantheon

The Pantheon is one of the most impressive and well-preserved ancient buildings in Rome. Here is a well-detailed guide to visiting the Pantheon:

Address: Piazza della Rotonda, 00186 Rome, Italy

- Open Google Maps on your device or computer.

- Type " **Pantheon** " into the search bar at the top of the screen.

- The map will show the location of the **Pantheon** in Rome, Italy, with a red marker.

- You can zoom in or out on the map to see the surrounding area and nearby attractions.

- To get directions to the **Pantheon** from your current location or another destination, click on the blue "Directions" button and enter your starting point or destination.

From there, you can use the map to navigate to the **Pantheon** and explore the surrounding area.

Other important travel details:

- Opening hours: The Pantheon is open every day from 9:00 AM to 7:30 PM. On holidays, the opening hours may vary.
- Admission: The Pantheon is free to enter.
- Dress code: As the Pantheon is a religious site, visitors are expected to dress modestly. Shorts, tank tops, and bare shoulders are not allowed.
- Photography: Photography is allowed inside the Pantheon, but the use of flash and tripods is prohibited.
- Guided tours: Guided tours of the Pantheon are available for a fee. You can book a tour in advance or join a group tour on the day of your visit.

Website: The official website of the Pantheon is not available as it is an ancient building, but you can find more information about the Pantheon on the official website of the Italian Ministry of Culture and Tourism: http://www.beniculturali.it/mibac/export/MiBAC/sito-MiBAC/Contenuti/MibacUnif/Eventi/visualizza_asset.html_2067877859.html

General tips to visit:

- Get there early: The Pantheon is a popular tourist attraction, so it can get crowded quickly. If you want to avoid the crowds, try to visit in the morning or early afternoon.
- Take your time: The Pantheon is a fascinating building with a lot of history and architectural features to explore. Take your time to appreciate the beauty of the building and its surroundings.
- Respect the site: As with all ancient buildings, it is important to respect the Pantheon and its history. Do not touch or climb on any of the structures and be mindful of the noise level.

Here are some additional details and information about The Pantheon:

History: The Pantheon was originally built as a temple to all the gods in ancient Rome around 126 AD by Emperor Hadrian. It was later converted into a Christian church in the 7th century and has been in continuous use since then.

Architecture: One of the most impressive features of the Pantheon is its dome, which was the largest unsupported dome in the world for over 1,300 years. The dome is made of concrete and has an oculus, or circular opening, at the top that lets in natural light. The building also has a portico with 16 granite columns and a bronze door.

Art and Decorations: Inside the Pantheon, you will find stunning artworks and decorations. The walls are lined with marble and have niches with statues of various gods and emperors. The floor is made of colorful marble and has a pattern of circles and squares. Above the entrance, there is an inscription in Latin that reads

"M·AGRIPPA·L·F·COS·TERTIVM·FECIT" ("Marcus Agrippa, son of Lucius, made [this building] when consul for the third time").

Famous Burials: The Pantheon is also the final resting place of several famous individuals, including the artist Raphael, the composer Arcangelo Corelli, and the first two kings of Italy, Victor Emmanuel II and Umberto I.

Interesting Facts:

- The Pantheon is a popular filming location and has been featured in several movies, including "Angels and Demons" and "Roman Holiday".
- The oculus in the dome of the Pantheon is not covered, which means that rain and snow can come inside the building. However, there is a drainage system in the floor to prevent flooding.
- The Pantheon is one of the most well-preserved ancient buildings in Rome and has survived earthquakes, fires, and wars.

Overall, The Pantheon is a must-visit attraction in Rome for anyone interested in history, art, and architecture. Its impressive dome, beautiful decorations, and fascinating history make it a truly unique and awe-inspiring experience.

Vatican City

here is a well-detailed guide to visiting Vatican City:

Location: Vatican City is located within the city of Rome, Italy. It is the smallest independent state in the world, covering an area of only 44 hectares (110 acres).

Vatican City is located on the west bank of the Tiber River and is surrounded by a high wall.

How to Get There: The most convenient way to get to Vatican City is by public transportation. You can take the metro to the Ottaviano-San Pietro station on Line A and then walk to Vatican City. Alternatively, you can take a bus or a taxi to the entrance of Vatican City.

Location on Google Maps: To locate Vatican City on Google Maps, simply type "Vatican City" into the search bar. The map will show the location of Vatican City in Rome.

Vatican City Website: The official website of Vatican City is www.vatican.va. This website provides information about the history, art, and culture of Vatican City, as well as information about visiting the Vatican Museums, St. Peter's Basilica, and other attractions.

Important Travel Tips:

1. Dress Code: Vatican City is a religious site and visitors are expected to dress modestly. Shorts, sleeveless tops, and mini-skirts are not allowed. Visitors who do not adhere to the dress code may be denied entry.
2. Security Checks: Visitors to Vatican City must pass through security checks, which can be time-consuming. It is recommended that you arrive early to allow enough time to go through security.
3. Tickets: To avoid long lines, it is recommended that you buy tickets in advance for attractions such as the Vatican Museums and St. Peter's Basilica. Tickets can be purchased on the official Vatican City website or at the entrance to the attractions.
4. Photography: Photography is allowed in most areas of Vatican City, but flash photography is prohibited in some areas. Be sure to check for signs indicating where photography is not allowed.

5. Guided Tours: Guided tours are available for the Vatican Museums, St. Peter's Basilica, and other attractions. These tours provide a wealth of information about the history and art of Vatican City.

Vatican City is a must-visit destination for anyone interested in history, art, and religion. Its stunning architecture, art collections, and religious significance make it a truly unique and unforgettable experience.

Here are some additional tips and details to enhance your visit to Vatican City:

- Plan your visit in advance: Vatican City is a popular destination, so it's a good idea to plan your visit in advance. You can purchase tickets online or through a tour company to skip the long lines and crowds. It's also a good idea to plan your visit during the off-season (October to March) to avoid the crowds.

- Wear comfortable shoes: Vatican City is a large complex with many attractions, so wear comfortable shoes to explore the area without feeling tired.

- Visit the Vatican Museums early in the morning: The Vatican Museums are one of the most popular attractions in Vatican City. If you want to avoid the crowds, plan to visit the museums early in the morning when they first open.

- Respect the rules and customs: Vatican City is a religious and cultural center, so it's important to respect the rules and customs. Dress modestly, avoid taking photos or videos where it's not allowed, and speak softly in the holy places.

By keeping these tips in mind, you can make the most of your visit to Vatican City and create memories that will last a lifetime.

Chapter 2

Planning Your Trip to Rome

When to Visit Rome and How to Get There:

Rome is a popular destination that attracts millions of tourists each year. Here's a guide to help you plan your trip:

When to Visit Rome: The best time to visit Rome is during the shoulder seasons, from April to May and from September to October. During these months, the weather is mild and the crowds are thinner than in the peak season. If you prefer warmer weather, you can visit in the summer months of June to August. However, it can be very hot, humid, and crowded during this time, so plan accordingly. Additionally, many locals take their summer vacation in August, so some shops and restaurants may be closed.

If you don't mind cooler weather, you can also visit Rome in the winter months from November to February. While it can be chilly, you can enjoy fewer crowds and lower prices.

How to Get There: Rome is served by two airports: Fiumicino Airport and Ciampino Airport. Fiumicino is the main airport and is located about 32 km from Rome's city center. You can reach the city by train, bus, or taxi. The Leonardo Express train departs every 15 minutes from the airport to Rome's Termini Station, the main railway station. The journey takes about 32 minutes and costs around 14 euros.

You can also take a bus from Fiumicino Airport to Rome's city center. The Terravision and Sit Bus Shuttle are popular options and cost around 5-7 euros. Taxis are available outside the airport but can be expensive, especially during peak hours.

Ciampino Airport is smaller and is mainly used by low-cost airlines. You can reach the city by bus, train or taxi. The Terravision and Sit Bus Shuttle also operate from this airport to Rome's city center.

If you prefer traveling by train, Rome's Termini Station is the main railway station and is well-connected to other Italian and European cities. High-speed trains from Florence, Milan, and Naples take about 1-3 hours.

If you're driving to Rome, be aware that traffic can be heavy and parking can be expensive. You can also take a coach bus from other Italian and European cities, but the journey can be longer than traveling by train.

Overall, Rome is easily accessible by air, train, or bus, and there are plenty of transportation options to get you around the city. Plan your trip according to the season that suits you best and choose a transportation option that works for your budget and schedule.

Accommodation options In Rome

Accommodation Options and How to Book Them in Rome:

Rome has a wide range of accommodation options to suit every budget and travel style, from luxury hotels to budget hostels. Here's a guide to help you choose the best option for your trip:

Hotels: Rome has a plethora of hotels that range from luxurious five-star accommodations to budget-friendly options. Some popular areas to stay in include the historic center, Trastevere, and the Vatican area.

Luxury hotels such as the Hotel Eden and the Hotel de Russie offer luxurious amenities such as spas, fine dining, and stunning views of the city. Mid-range options such as the Hotel Santa Maria in

Trastevere offer comfortable rooms and a convenient location.

To book a hotel in Rome, you can use popular booking websites such as Booking.com, Expedia, or Hotels.com. Alternatively, you can book directly through the hotel's website. Keep in mind that prices can vary depending on the season, so it's best to book in advance to secure the best deal.

Hostels: If you're on a budget, hostels are a great option for affordable accommodation in Rome. Hostels such as the Yellow Hostel and the Alessandro Palace Hostel offer dormitory-style accommodation as well as private rooms.

Hostels can be booked through popular booking websites such as Hostelworld and Booking.com, or directly through the hostel's website. Prices vary depending on the season and the type of accommodation.

Airbnb: Another popular option for accommodation in Rome is Airbnb, which offers a wide range of apartments and rooms for rent. This option is great for those who want a more local experience and prefer the privacy of their own space.

To book an Airbnb in Rome, you can search for available properties on the Airbnb website or app. Prices vary depending on the season of the year and the location of the property.

here are the best hotels in Rome, along with their addresses, locations, websites, and prices:

1. **Hotel Eden** Address: Via Ludovisi 49, 00187 Rome, Italy Location: This luxurious hotel is located in the heart of Rome, just a short walk from the Spanish Steps and the Trevi Fountain. Website: https://www.dorchestercollection.com/en/rome/hotel-eden/ Price: Starting from €670 per night

Pros: Hotel Eden offers stunning views of the city and features elegant decor, a rooftop restaurant, and an indoor pool.

Cons: This hotel is quite expensive and may not be affordable for all travelers.

2. **Hotel Hassler Roma ,** Address**:** Piazza della Trinita dei Monti 6, 00187 Rome, Italy Location: Situated at the top of the Spanish Steps, Hotel Hassler Roma offers panoramic views of the city. Website: https://www.hotelhasslerroma.com/ Price: Starting from €515 per night

Pros: The hotel features a Michelin-starred restaurant, a rooftop bar, and luxurious rooms with marble bathrooms.

Cons: The hotel's prime location can make it quite noisy, especially during peak tourist season.

3. Portrait Roma Address: Via Bocca di Leone 23, 00187 Rome, Italy Location: This chic hotel is located in the center of Rome, just

a short walk from the Spanish Steps and Via dei Condotti shopping street. Website: https://www.lungarnocollection.com/portrait-roma Price: Starting from €550 per night

Pros: The hotel offers spacious, stylish suites with private terraces, as well as a rooftop bar and restaurant.

Cons: Some guests have noted that the hotel's street-facing rooms can be noisy.

4. **Hotel de Russie ,** Address**:** Via del Babuino 9, 00187 Rome, Italy Location: This elegant hotel is located in the historic center of Rome, just a few minutes' walk from the Spanish Steps and the Villa Borghese gardens. Website: https://www.roccofortehotels.com/hotels-and-resorts/hotel-de-russie/ Price: Starting from €500 per night

Pros: Hotel de Russie features a beautiful garden terrace, a Michelin-starred restaurant, and spacious, stylish rooms.

Cons: The hotel's prime location can make it quite noisy, and some guests have noted that the rooms can be a bit dark.

5. **J.K. Place Roma ,** **Address:** Via di Monte d'Oro 30, 00186 Rome, Italy Location: This stylish hotel is located in the heart of Rome, just a short walk from the Spanish Steps and the Pantheon. Website: https://www.jkroma.com/ Price: Starting from €600 per night

   Pros: J.K. Place Roma features elegant, individually decorated rooms, as well as a rooftop bar and restaurant.

   Cons: The hotel is quite expensive and may not be affordable for all travelers.

   To locate these hotels using Google Maps, simply type in the hotel name or address in the search bar, and the location should appear on the map. From there, you can easily navigate to the hotel using your preferred mode of transportation.

Here are the best hostels in Rome, their addresses, locations, websites, prices, and pros and cons:

1. **The Yellow Hostel ,** Address: Via Palestro, 44, 00185 Roma RM, Italy Location: The Yellow Hostel is located in the central area of Rome, a 10-minute walk from Termini Station. Website: https://www.the-yellow.com/ Price: Dorm beds start from €25 per night. Pros: The Yellow Hostel is known for its lively atmosphere, with a bar and a nightclub on-site. The hostel also offers a variety of events and activities, such as pub crawls and walking tours. The staff is friendly and helpful, and the facilities are clean and well-maintained. Cons: Due to the lively atmosphere, it may not be the best choice for those looking for a quiet and peaceful stay. Some guests have complained about noise levels in the rooms.

2. **Alessandro Palace Hostel & Bar ,** Address: Via Vicenza, 42, 00185 Roma RM,

Italy Location: Alessandro Palace Hostel & Bar is located near Termini Station, in the heart of Rome. Website: https://www.alessandro-palace.com/ Price: Dorm beds start from €20 per night. Pros: The hostel offers a variety of services, including free Wi-Fi, a bar, and a restaurant. The staff is friendly and knowledgeable about the city, and can provide tips and recommendations. The rooms are clean and comfortable, with lockers and personal reading lights. Cons: Some guests have complained about noise levels, as the hostel is located on a busy street. The breakfast is not included in the room rate and must be purchased separately.

3. **Generator Rome**, Address: Via Principe Amedeo, 251, 00185 Roma RM, Italy Location: Generator Rome is located near Termini Station, in the lively Esquilino neighborhood. Website:

https://staygenerator.com/hostels/rome
Price: Dorm beds start from €20 per night. Pros: The hostel features modern and stylish design, with a rooftop terrace and a bar. The staff is friendly and helpful, and the facilities are clean and well-maintained. The hostel also offers a variety of events and activities, such as live music and art exhibitions. Cons: Some guests have complained about noise levels in the rooms. The hostel is a bit far from the city center and most attractions.

4. **Hostel Alessandro Downtown ,** Address: Via Carlo Cattaneo, 23, 00185 Roma RM, Italy Location: Hostel Alessandro Downtown is located near Termini Station, in the heart of Rome. Website: https://www.alessandro-downtown.com/ Price: Dorm beds start from €18 per night. Pros: The hostel offers a variety of services, including free Wi-Fi, a bar, and a lounge area. The staff is friendly and knowledgeable about the city, and can provide tips and recommendations. The

rooms are clean and comfortable, with lockers and personal reading lights. Cons: Some guests have complained about noise levels, as the hostel is located on a busy street. The breakfast is not included in the room rate and must be purchased separately.

5. **Roma Scout Center ,** Address: Largo dello Scautismo, 1, 00162 Roma RM, Italy Location: Roma Scout Center is located in the Nomentano neighborhood, a bit farther from the city center. Website: https://www.romascoutcenter.it/ Price: Dorm beds start from €19 per night. Pros: The hostel offers a peaceful and relaxing atmosphere, with a garden and a terrace. The staff is friendly and helpful, and the facilities are

How to Locate Accommodations Using Google Maps in rome

Google Maps is an essential tool when it comes to locating accommodations in Rome. It is an easy and efficient way to find the address and location of your desired accommodation. Here is a detailed guide on how to locate accommodations using Google Maps in Rome.

1. Open Google Maps: Start by opening the Google Maps app on your phone or computer. If you don't have the app, you can download it from the App Store or Google Play Store.
2. Enter the address: Once you open the app, type in the address of your desired accommodation in Rome. You can also search for the name of the accommodation or the area you want to stay in.
3. Zoom in: Once you have entered the address, zoom in on the map to get a better look at the location. You can also

use the street view feature to get a closer look at the surroundings.
4. Check the surrounding area: Take a look at the surrounding area to see what is nearby. Check for restaurants, cafes, shops, and public transport links. This will help you get a better idea of what to expect in the area.
5. Check reviews and ratings: Once you have located the accommodation on Google Maps, you can check the reviews and ratings to get an idea of what other people thought of their stay. This can help you make an informed decision when choosing where to stay.
6. Save the location: Once you have found the location of the accommodation, you can save it on Google Maps for future reference. This will make it easier to find the location again if you need to refer to it later.
7. Get directions: Finally, you can use Google Maps to get directions to the accommodation. Simply enter your current location and the app will provide you with directions to your destination.

In conclusion, using Google Maps to locate accommodations in Rome is an easy and efficient way to find the address and location of your desired accommodation. By following these simple steps, you can easily locate accommodations and make an informed decision when choosing where to stay.

Budgeting and money-saving tips for Rome

Rome is known to be one of the most expensive cities in Europe, but with some planning and budgeting, you can enjoy all the sights and sounds without breaking the bank. Here are some budgeting and money-saving tips for Rome:

1. Visit during the offseason: The peak season in Rome is from June to August, which means higher prices for accommodation, food, and attractions. Visiting during the offseason, from November to February, can save you a lot of money.

2. Use public transportation: Rome has an efficient public transportation system that includes buses, metro, and trams. Buying a multi-day pass or a Roma Pass can save you a lot of money compared to buying individual tickets.

3. Walk as much as possible: Rome is a walkable city, and walking around can save you money on transportation costs. Walking also allows you to explore the city at your own pace and discover hidden gems that you might not have found otherwise.

4. Eat like a local: Avoid eating in the tourist areas as they tend to be more expensive. Look for local restaurants and trattorias, where the locals eat. You'll get an authentic experience and save money at the same time.

5. Drink tap water: Rome has some of the cleanest tap water in Europe, so there's no need to buy bottled water. Bring a refillable water bottle and fill up at one of the many public drinking fountains throughout the city.

6. Take advantage of free attractions: Rome has many free attractions, including the Pantheon, the Trevi Fountain, and the Spanish Steps. You can also visit many of the city's beautiful churches for free.

7. Book in advance: Booking tours, attractions, and accommodations in advance can often save you money. Look for deals and discounts online and compare prices before making a purchase.

8. Stay in a budget-friendly accommodation: Hostels and budget hotels can be found throughout Rome, offering affordable

accommodation options. Consider staying in a hostel or budget hotel to save money on your trip.

9. Avoid unnecessary expenses: Rome is full of tempting souvenirs, but buying too many can quickly add up. Stick to a budget and avoid overspending on unnecessary items.

By following these budgeting and money-saving tips for Rome, you can enjoy all that this beautiful city has to offer without breaking the bank.

Here are some additional tips for budgeting and saving money while visiting Rome:

1. Plan your meals wisely: Eating out in Rome can be quite expensive, especially in touristy areas. To save money, opt for local food markets or street food vendors where you can find delicious and affordable

meals. You can also consider booking accommodations that include breakfast to save money on your morning meal.

2. Use public transportation: Rome has a great public transportation system, including buses, trams, and metros. Purchase a multi-day pass to save money on transportation costs, rather than buying individual tickets.

3. Visit free attractions: While Rome is known for its many historical and cultural attractions, there are also plenty of free things to see and do. Visit attractions like the Trevi Fountain, Spanish Steps, and Pantheon, which are all free to visit.

4. Avoid peak season: Rome can be extremely crowded during peak season, which is typically from June to August. To save money on accommodations and avoid long

lines, consider visiting during the off-season, such as in the spring or fall.

5. Shop smart: If you're interested in shopping while in Rome, avoid the touristy areas and instead head to local markets or shops. You can find unique souvenirs and gifts at a lower cost.

By following these tips, you can save money and still have an amazing time exploring all that Rome has to offer.

Chapter 3

Exploring Ancient Rome

The Colosseum and Roman Forum are two of Rome's most iconic ancient attractions. Here's a guide on how to explore and visit them:

Here is a well-detailed guide on how to make the most out of your visit to these historical landmarks.

1. Understanding the history:

The Colosseum and Roman Forum are both iconic symbols of ancient Rome, and visiting them provides an opportunity to learn about the history of the Roman Empire. The Colosseum was built in AD 80 and is considered one of the greatest engineering feats of the ancient world. It was used for gladiator games, public spectacles, and other events. The Roman

Forum, located nearby, was the center of political and social life in ancient Rome.

2. Planning your visit:

To make the most out of your visit to the Colosseum and Roman Forum, it's recommended to buy tickets in advance to avoid long queues. You can also purchase combination tickets that include access to other nearby attractions, such as the Palatine Hill. It's also important to note that the Colosseum and Roman Forum are closed on Mondays.

3. Visiting the Colosseum:

When you arrive at the Colosseum, it's recommended to join a guided tour to fully appreciate its history and significance. Audio guides are also available. Make sure to wear comfortable shoes as there is a lot of walking involved, and bring water as it can get hot during the summer months. It's important to note that there are security checks before entering the Colosseum, so make sure to leave any prohibited items such as sharp objects or large bags at your accommodation.

4. Exploring the Roman Forum:

    After visiting the Colosseum, head over to the Roman Forum, which is just a short walk away. The Roman Forum is a vast complex of ruins that was once the center of political and social life in ancient Rome. It's recommended to join a guided tour or hire an audio guide to fully appreciate the history and significance of the ruins. Some of the highlights include the Temple of Saturn, the Arch of Titus, and the House of the Vestal Virgins.

5. General tips:

    To make the most out of your visit to the Colosseum and Roman Forum, here are some general tips:

- Arrive early in the morning to avoid crowds and long queues.

- Wear comfortable shoes and bring water.
- Consider joining a guided tour or hiring an audio guide to fully appreciate the history and significance of the sites.
- Respect the historical significance of the sites and refrain from touching or climbing on any of the ruins.
- Take plenty of photos to remember your visit to these iconic landmarks.

Exploring The Roman Forum

The Roman Forum is an archaeological site in the center of Rome that was the social, commercial, and political hub of ancient Rome. Visiting the Roman Forum provides a glimpse into the heart of the Roman Empire, and is a must-see for any history lover or traveler visiting Rome. Here's a guide on how to visit the Roman Forum:

Address: Via della Salara Vecchia, 5/6, 00186 Rome, Italy

Location: The Roman Forum is located in the center of Rome, between the Palatine Hill and the Capitoline Hill. The entrance to the Roman Forum is located on Via dei Fori Imperiali.

How to Get There: The Roman Forum is easily accessible by public transportation. The closest metro station is Colosseo on Line B. The site can also be reached by bus or tram. It is recommended to use public transportation as parking can be limited in the area.

Ticket Prices: A combined ticket for the Roman Forum, Colosseum, and Palatine Hill costs €16 for adults, €2 for EU citizens between 18-25 years old, and free for children under 18. It is recommended to purchase tickets in advance online or at the ticket office to avoid long lines.

Hours: The Roman Forum is open every day from 8:30 am to one hour before sunset. It is closed on January 1st and December 25th.

Website: http://archeoroma.beniculturali.it/en/archaeological-site/roman-forum-and-palatine-hill

General Travel Tips:

1. Wear comfortable shoes as there is a lot of walking and uneven terrain at the Roman Forum.
2. Consider hiring a guide or audio guide to enhance your experience and learn more about the history and significance of the site.
3. Bring water and snacks, as there are limited food options available at the Roman Forum.
4. Plan to spend at least 2-3 hours at the Roman Forum to fully explore the site and take in its history and beauty.
5. Respect the site and its artifacts by not touching or climbing on any ruins.
6. The site can be crowded, especially during peak tourist season, so plan accordingly and arrive early to avoid crowds.

Website to book ticket for Roman Forum

The official website to book tickets for the Roman Forum and other archaeological sites in Rome is www.coopculture.it. You can also book tickets for the Roman Forum on other third-party websites such as www.viator.com or www.tiqets.com. It is recommended to book your tickets in advance, especially during peak tourist seasons, to avoid long queues and ensure availability.

Exploring the Palatine Hill and Circus Maximus

When visiting Rome, don't miss the opportunity to explore the Palatine Hill and Circus Maximus. These two ancient sites are rich in history and offer visitors a unique glimpse into ancient Rome.

Palatine Hill:

The Palatine Hill is one of the Seven Hills of Rome and is considered to be the birthplace of the city. It is said that Romulus and Remus, the legendary founders of Rome, were found here by a she-wolf. The hill is home to the ruins of several ancient palaces, including the Palace of Domitian and the Palace of Augustus.

Address: Via di San Gregorio, 30, 00186 Roma RM, Italy

Location on the map:

How to locate on Google Maps: Type in "Palatine Hill" and it will appear on the map. Alternatively, use the address provided above to navigate to the site.

Website: https://www.coopculture.it/en/heritage.cfm?id=4

General Travel Tips to Palatine Hill:

1. Buy tickets in advance: You can purchase tickets online or at the ticket office on-site.

2. Wear comfortable shoes: The Palatine Hill is quite large and has uneven terrain, so comfortable shoes are a must.
3. Guided tours: Consider taking a guided tour to learn more about the history and significance of the site.
4. Plan your visit: The Palatine Hill is open every day except for Christmas Day and New Year's Day. We recommend checking

the website for opening times and any special events that may be taking place.

Circus Maximus:

The Circus Maximus is an ancient chariot racing stadium located between the Aventine and Palatine Hills. It was the largest stadium in ancient Rome and could hold up to 150,000 spectators. Today, the site is a peaceful public park with little evidence of its former glory.

Address: Via del Circo Massimo, 00186 Roma RM, Italy

Location on the map:

How to locate on Google Maps: Type in "Circus Maximus" and it will appear on the map. Alternatively, use the address provided above to navigate to the site.

Website: https://www.coopculture.it/en/heritage.cfm?id=6

General Travel Tips to Circus Maximus:

1. Visit early or late: The site can get quite crowded during peak hours, so we recommend visiting early in the morning or later in the evening.
2. Bring water: The park has limited facilities, so bring your own water and snacks.
3. Take a walk: The park is a great place to take a leisurely walk and enjoy the views of ancient Rome.
4. Check for events: The Circus Maximus is still used for events today, so check the website for any upcoming concerts or festivals.

Learning about the history and architecture of ancient Rome

Rome is one of the most historically significant cities in the world. It is known for its rich history and remarkable architecture, particularly from the ancient Roman period. A visit to Rome is incomplete without exploring the history and architecture of ancient Rome.

The history of ancient Rome dates back to 753 BC when it was founded. It was once the capital of the Roman Empire, which spanned from Europe to the Middle East and North Africa. The Roman Empire was known for its military prowess, engineering, and cultural advancements. Some of the most significant historical events that took place in ancient Rome include the assassination of Julius Caesar, the rise and fall of the Roman Empire, and the emergence of Christianity.

One of the most remarkable architectural achievements of ancient Rome is the Colosseum. It was built between 72-80 AD and is one of the largest amphitheaters in the world. The Colosseum is a testament to the engineering and architectural achievements of ancient Rome.

The Pantheon is another remarkable ancient Roman structure that is still standing. It was built between 118-128 AD as a temple to all the gods. It is known for its impressive dome and is considered a masterpiece of ancient engineering.

The Roman Forum is another must-visit destination for those interested in ancient Roman history and architecture. It was once the center of political and social activities in ancient Rome.

The forum is home to many ruins, including the Temple of Saturn, the Arch of Septimius Severus, and the Temple of Vesta.

The Palatine Hill is another important historical site in Rome. It was once the site of the Imperial Palace and is now home to many impressive ruins, including the Domus Augustana, the Stadium of Domitian, and the House of Livia.

If you are interested in learning more about ancient Rome, there are several museums in Rome dedicated to the history and culture of ancient Rome. The Capitoline Museums, for example, house many important artifacts from ancient Rome, including the Capitoline Wolf, the symbol of Rome.

Overall, a visit to Rome is incomplete without exploring the history and architecture of ancient Rome. From the Colosseum to the Pantheon, the Roman Forum to the Palatine Hill, there is much to see and learn about this remarkable period in human history.

Rome is a city steeped in history, and one of the most important periods of its past is the Renaissance. This period of artistic and cultural growth began in the 14th century in Italy and spread throughout Europe, leaving an indelible mark on Rome's architecture and art. Visitors to Rome can discover this rich legacy through its art and architecture.

One of the most iconic Renaissance buildings in Rome is the Palazzo Farnese. Originally built for a noble family in the 16th century, the palace now houses the French Embassy in Italy. Visitors can admire its stunning architecture, including its magnificent central courtyard and grand staircase. Guided tours are available for those who want to learn more about the palace's history and art.

Another must-see Renaissance masterpiece in Rome is the Villa Farnesina. Built for a wealthy banker in the early 16th century, this villa is home to some of the most beautiful frescoes in Rome. Painted by Renaissance masters such as Raphael and

Sebastiano del Piombo, the frescoes depict scenes from classical mythology and the Bible. Visitors can take a guided tour to learn more about the villa's history and the art on display.

For those interested in Renaissance art, the Galleria Borghese is a must-visit. Housed in a beautiful villa in the heart of Rome, the gallery boasts an impressive collection of Renaissance and Baroque art. Visitors can admire masterpieces by Caravaggio, Bernini, and Raphael, among others. It is recommended to book tickets in advance, as the gallery is very popular and has a limited number of visitors allowed each day.

The Piazza del Campidoglio is another must-see destination for lovers of Renaissance art and architecture. Designed by Michelangelo in the 16th century, the piazza features a magnificent staircase leading up to the Palazzo Senatorio, which now houses the city hall. Visitors can admire the statue of Marcus Aurelius, the only equestrian statue from ancient Rome to have survived to the present day.

Visitors can also explore the churches of Rome to discover the city's Renaissance art. The Chiesa di Santa Maria del Popolo, for example, houses works by Caravaggio and Raphael. The Basilica di Santa Maria degli Angeli e dei Martiri, located in the Baths of Diocletian, features a stunning meridian line designed by the Renaissance scientist and artist Gianlorenzo Bernini.

In conclusion, Rome is a city that offers a rich and diverse array of art and architecture, with the Renaissance period playing a significant role in its history. Visitors can explore the city's museums, galleries, and churches to discover its artistic legacy, and gain a deeper appreciation of the cultural richness of Rome.

Chapter 4

Discovering the Art and Architecture of Rome

Discovering the Renaissance art and architecture of Rome can be a wonderful experience for history and art lovers. Here are some of the top places to visit in Rome to explore Renaissance art and architecture:

1. **Villa Borghese:** This beautiful villa is home to the Borghese Gallery, which houses an impressive collection of Renaissance art, including works by Raphael, Caravaggio, and Bernini.

Address: Piazzale del Museo Borghese, 00197 Rome, Italy Website: https://galleriaborghese.beniculturali.it/

2. **Palazzo Farnese:** This grand Renaissance palace was built in the 16th century and now houses the

French Embassy. Visitors can admire the beautiful architecture and frescoes by famous Renaissance artists such as Annibale Carracci.

Address: Piazza Farnese, 00186 Rome, Italy

3. Capitoline Museums: The Capitoline Museums house an impressive collection of Renaissance art, including works by artists such as Titian, Caravaggio, and Raphael. The museum is also known for its stunning Renaissance architecture.

Address: Piazza del Campidoglio, 1, 00186 Rome, Italy Website: https://www.museicapitolini.org/en/

When visiting these sites, it's important to check the opening hours and book tickets in advance to avoid long queues. Many of these attractions offer guided tours or audio guides to enhance your experience. It's also important to dress appropriately, as some churches and museums may have dress codes. Finally, be sure to bring a camera to capture the beauty of these historic landmarks.

Chapter 5

Rome's Neighborhoods and Local Culture

Exploring Trastevere, the Jewish Ghetto, and other unique neighborhoods in Rome is a great way to experience the local culture and get a taste of authentic Roman life. Each neighborhood has its own distinct character and attractions, from charming cobblestone streets to hidden alleys lined with local eateries and artisan shops.

Trastevere, located on the west bank of the Tiber River, is known for its lively atmosphere, bohemian vibe, and bustling nightlife. The neighborhood is home to many restaurants, bars, and cafes, making it a popular destination for both locals and tourists. The picturesque Piazza di Santa Maria in Trastevere is the heart of the neighborhood and a great place to grab a drink or a bite to eat while people-watching.

The Jewish Ghetto is located in the heart of Rome, between the Tiber River and the Campo de' Fiori market. This historic neighborhood has a rich cultural heritage and is home to several famous landmarks, including the Great Synagogue of Rome, the Jewish Museum, and the Fontana delle Tartarughe. The area is also known for its delicious kosher cuisine, which can be found in the many restaurants and cafes that line the narrow streets.

Other unique neighborhoods worth exploring in Rome include Monti, known for its vintage shops and trendy bars, and Testaccio, a former working-class neighborhood that has since transformed into a foodie destination with some of the best restaurants in the city.

To explore these neighborhoods, it's best to take a leisurely walk and soak in the sights, sounds, and smells. Rome is a very walkable city, and many of the neighborhoods are easily accessible by foot or by public transportation. It's also a good idea to research any special events or festivals that may be happening in these neighborhoods, as they can provide a unique and memorable experience.

Finally, don't forget to sample the local cuisine and wine in these neighborhoods. Each neighborhood has its own specialties and culinary traditions, and trying new foods and drinks is an important part of experiencing the local culture. So whether it's a classic Roman dish like cacio e pepe or a glass of crisp white wine from the nearby Frascati region, be sure to indulge in the flavors of Rome's unique neighborhoods.

Sampling local Roman cuisine and wine

When visiting Rome, one of the most important experiences is to sample the delicious local cuisine and wine. Roman cuisine is known for its simplicity, using fresh ingredients and traditional cooking methods to create flavorful dishes. From classic pasta dishes to hearty meat and fish dishes, there is something for every taste in Rome.

Here are some tips on how to sample local Roman cuisine and wine:

1. Visit Local Markets: One of the best ways to experience local cuisine is by visiting local markets such as Campo de' Fiori, Mercato Trionfale, or Testaccio Market. Here you can find fresh produce, meats, cheeses, and other local specialties. Many markets also have small food stalls where you can taste local dishes.

2. Try Roman Street Food: Rome is known for its delicious street food such as suppli (fried rice balls), pizza al taglio (pizza by the slice), and porchetta (roasted pork). You can find these delicacies at small food stands around the city.

3. Eat Like a Roman: When dining out, try ordering traditional Roman dishes such as amatriciana (pasta with tomato sauce, guanciale, and pecorino cheese), cacio e pepe (pasta with pecorino cheese and black pepper), and saltimbocca alla romana (veal cutlets with prosciutto and sage). Also, be sure to try local specialties such as carciofi alla giudia (Jewish-style artichokes) and abbacchio alla scottadito (grilled lamb chops).

4. Sample Local Wines: Rome is surrounded by beautiful vineyards, and there are many local wines to sample. Look for wines from the Lazio region, such as Frascati and Castelli Romani, which are crisp and refreshing white wines. Also, try the bold and full-bodied red wines from the nearby region of Tuscany.

5. Take a Food Tour: To get a more in-depth understanding of Roman cuisine, consider taking a food tour. These tours take you to local markets, restaurants, and food stands, where you can sample a variety of dishes and learn about the history and culture behind them.

In addition to sampling local cuisine, be sure to also enjoy the local wine and spirits. Romans enjoy aperitivo, a pre-dinner drink and snack, and often enjoy wine with meals. There are many local bars and wine shops where you can sample different wines and spirits.

Overall, sampling local cuisine and wine is an essential part of any trip to Rome. Be sure to explore the markets, try street food, dine like a local, sample local wines, and take a food tour to truly experience the flavors of Rome.

Local markets in rome

Here is a guide to the top local markets in Rome:

1. **Campo de' Fiori Market** - located in the heart of Rome's historic center, this market is open every morning except Sunday. Here you can find fresh fruits and vegetables, meats, cheeses, and specialty foods like truffles and olives. There are also stalls selling souvenirs and other items.

   Address: Piazza Campo de' Fiori, 00186 Rome, Italy Open hours: Monday-Saturday from 7:00am to 2:00pm

   Tourist tips: This market can get quite crowded, so arrive early to beat the crowds. Also, be prepared to bargain with the vendors for better prices.

2. **Mercato Centrale** - located in the Termini train station, this market offers a modern twist on traditional Italian markets. There are over 20 stalls selling fresh ingredients

for cooking, as well as prepared foods and wine.

Address: Via Giolitti, 36, 00185 Rome, Italy
Open hours: Daily from 8:00am to midnight

Tourist tips: This market is a bit more upscale and expensive than other local markets, so it's a good option if you're looking for higher quality ingredients.

3. **Testaccio Market** - located in the Testaccio neighborhood, this market is known for its selection of meats, cheeses, and fresh produce. It's also a great place to sample traditional Roman dishes like pasta alla carbonara and coda alla vaccinara.

Address: Via Beniamino Franklin, 12/E, 00153 Rome, Italy Open hours: Monday-Saturday from 7:00am to 3:30pm

Tourist tips: This market is popular with locals, so be prepared to navigate through crowds. Also, many of the vendors only speak Italian, so brush up on your language skills before you go.

4. **Mercato di Via Portuense** - located in the Monteverde neighborhood, this market offers a wide range of fresh fruits and vegetables, as well as meats and cheeses. It's also a great place to find affordable clothing and household items.

   Address: Via Portuense, 1645, 00148 Rome, Italy Open hours: Monday-Saturday from 7:00am to 2:00pm

   Tourist tips: This market is less touristy than others in Rome, so it's a great option if you're looking for an authentic local experience. However, it's a bit further from the city center, so plan your transportation accordingly.

5. **Mercato di Testaccio** - located in the Testaccio neighborhood, this market is known for its fresh produce, meats, and seafood. There are also stalls selling street food, as well as wines and specialty foods.

Address: Via Galvani, 28, 00153 Rome, Italy
Open hours: Monday-Saturday from 7:00am to 3:30pm

Tourist tips: This market is popular with locals, so it's a great place to experience authentic Roman culture. However, it can get crowded, so arrive early to beat the crowds.

Experiencing Rome's nightlife and entertainment scene

Rome is not only famous for its historical sites and cultural attractions but also for its lively and vibrant nightlife. The city has a wide range of entertainment options to offer visitors, including bars, nightclubs, music venues, and cultural events. Here's a guide on experiencing Rome's nightlife and entertainment scene.

1. Piazza Navona: One of Rome's most famous squares, Piazza Navona is a

popular spot for nightlife. The square has a great atmosphere with street performers, cafes, and restaurants. The bars and cafes here are perfect for a relaxing drink or a romantic evening out.

2. Campo de' Fiori: This bustling square is a hub for nightlife, especially for young people. The area is full of bars and nightclubs that cater to all types of music and tastes. You can find everything from jazz clubs to techno clubs here.

3. Trastevere: Located on the west bank of the Tiber River, Trastevere is a bohemian neighborhood that comes alive at night. This is the perfect place to experience the local nightlife scene. There are many bars, cafes, and restaurants where you can enjoy a drink, listen to music, and mingle with the locals.
4. Testaccio: Testaccio is a neighborhood that is famous for its nightlife. The area is full of

bars, clubs, and discos, and it is a popular spot for party-goers. The clubs here are known for their techno and electronic music.

5. Auditorium Parco della Musica: This is one of Rome's most important music venues, hosting a variety of concerts and events throughout the year. The auditorium has three concert halls, and it is home to the Accademia Nazionale di Santa Cecilia, one of Italy's most prestigious music schools.

6. Teatro dell'Opera: If you are interested in theater, this is the place to be. The Teatro dell'Opera is one of Rome's most important theaters, and it hosts a variety of shows and performances throughout the year.

7. Food and Wine Tasting: Rome is famous for its food and wine, and there are many places where you can sample local cuisine

and wine. You can take a food tour of the city, visit a local market, or take a cooking class to learn how to make your own pasta and sauces.

General Travel Tips:

- Rome's nightlife scene starts late, with most bars and clubs opening around 11 pm and staying open until the early hours of the morning.
- Dress code varies from place to place, but it's always a good idea to dress smart-casual if you're going out at night.
- Be aware of pickpockets, especially in crowded areas and public transportation.
- Taxis can be expensive, so it's a good idea to use public transportation or walk.
- Don't forget to try the local drinks like Aperol Spritz, Negroni, and Prosecco while enjoying the nightlife.

Overall, Rome has a diverse and exciting nightlife scene that can cater to all types of visitors. Whether you want to dance the night away or enjoy a relaxing drink in a cozy bar, there is something for everyone in Rome's nightlife and entertainment scene.

Sure, here are some important details for experiencing Rome's nightlife:

1. Campo de' Fiori: This historic square is known for its lively atmosphere and numerous bars and restaurants. It's a popular spot for locals and tourists alike, especially in the evenings. Address: Piazza Campo de' Fiori, 00186 Rome, Italy.

2. Trastevere: This neighborhood is known for its vibrant nightlife, with numerous bars, clubs, and live music venues. Some popular spots include Freni e Frizioni, Ma Che Siete Venuti a Fa, and Rome's Comedy Club. Address: Trastevere, Rome, Italy.

3. Testaccio: This neighborhood has a more alternative and edgy nightlife scene, with

clubs and bars catering to a younger crowd. Some popular spots include Akab, Caffè Latino, and the Ex Dogana cultural center. Address: Testaccio, Rome, Italy.

4. Ostiense: This neighborhood has a mix of traditional and modern bars and clubs, with a focus on live music and DJ sets. Some popular spots include Goa Club, Lanificio 159, and Porto Fluviale. Address: Ostiense, Rome, Italy.

5. Monti: This trendy neighborhood has a bohemian vibe and is home to numerous bars and clubs. Some popular spots include Black Market, La Bottega del Caffè, and the intimate jazz club Gregory's. Address: Monti, Rome, Italy. Website: N/A.

It's important to note that many bars and clubs in Rome have a dress code, so be sure to dress appropriately. Additionally, it's recommended to avoid tourist traps and instead seek out local recommendations for the best nightlife experiences. Finally, be sure to practice responsible drinking and stay aware of your surroundings.

Chapter 6

Practical Information for Visiting Rome

Rome is a beautiful city, rich in history and culture, and attracts millions of visitors every year. As with any popular tourist destination, it's important to be aware of some essential travel tips to ensure your trip is enjoyable and safe. Here are some tips for transportation and safety in Rome:

Transportation:

1. Walk or take public transportation: Rome is a city best explored on foot or by taking public transportation. The historic center of Rome is a restricted traffic zone (ZTL), and only authorized vehicles are allowed to drive there. Walking is the best way to explore the city, but if you need to take transportation, use the bus, tram or metro.

2. Buy a transportation pass: If you're planning on using public transportation frequently, consider buying a transportation pass. There are different types of passes available, depending on the length of your stay and the zones you want to travel in.

3. Taxis: If you need to take a taxi, make sure it's an authorized taxi. Authorized taxis are white and have a taxi sign on the roof, a meter, and the license number displayed on the doors. Avoid unlicensed taxis or drivers who offer you a ride on the street.

4. Renting a car: It's not recommended to rent a car in Rome, especially if you're not used to driving in a busy city with narrow streets. If you must rent a car, make sure to get an International Driving Permit and have a GPS device to help navigate the streets.

Safety:

1. Watch out for pickpockets: Like in any big city, pickpocketing is a common problem in Rome. Keep your valuables close to you, avoid carrying large amounts of cash, and be aware of your surroundings in crowded areas.
2. Be cautious at night: While Rome is generally a safe city, it's important to be cautious at night, especially in less crowded areas. Avoid walking alone at night, and if you must, stick to well-lit areas.
3. Be respectful of local customs: Rome is a city with a rich history and culture, and it's important to be respectful of local customs and traditions. Dress modestly when visiting churches or religious sites, and avoid loud or disruptive behavior in public places.
4. Be aware of traffic: Traffic in Rome can be chaotic, and drivers often ignore traffic signals and rules. Be aware when crossing the street and always use pedestrian crossings.

By following these essential travel tips for transportation and safety in Rome, you can ensure that your trip is enjoyable and stress-free.

Additional tips for transportation and safety in Rome:

1. Be aware of pickpockets: Rome is notorious for pickpocketing, especially in crowded areas like public transportation, tourist attractions, and busy streets. Keep your valuables close and be cautious of anyone who seems to be trying to distract you.
2. Use public transportation: Rome has a good public transportation system, including buses, trams, and a subway. The most convenient way to use public transportation is by purchasing a daily or weekly pass, which allows for unlimited travel on all modes of transportation.

3. Walk when possible: Rome is a very walkable city, and walking is often the best way to explore the city's charming

neighborhoods and discover hidden gems. Plus, walking is free and can save you money on transportation costs.

4. Use taxis with caution: Taxis in Rome can be expensive and some drivers have been known to overcharge tourists. Always use licensed taxis, which are white and have a "TAXI" sign on the roof, and make sure the meter is running.

5. Be mindful of traffic: Rome's streets can be chaotic, and traffic can be heavy at certain times of the day. Pedestrians do not always have the right of way, so be careful when crossing streets.

6. Dress appropriately: If you plan to visit churches or other religious sites, be sure to dress appropriately, covering your shoulders and knees. This is a sign of respect and is required in many religious sites.

7. Stay hydrated: Rome can be hot and humid, especially in the summer months. Be sure to drink plenty of water and carry a refillable water bottle with you to stay hydrated.
8. Know emergency numbers: In case of an emergency, the emergency number in Italy is 112. It is also a good idea to have the contact information for your embassy or consulate on hand.

By following these tips, you can have a safe and enjoyable visit to Rome.

Common Italian phrases and customs to know

If you're planning a trip to Rome, it's always a good idea to brush up on some common Italian phrases and customs. Not only will it make your trip more enjoyable, but it's also a great way to show respect for the local culture. Here are some common

Italian phrases and customs to know before your trip:

1. Greetings: It's always polite to greet someone in Italian, especially if you're asking for directions or ordering food. The most common greeting is "Ciao" (pronounced "chow"), which means both "hello" and "goodbye". Another common greeting is "Buongiorno" (pronounced "bwohn-jor-no"), which means "good morning" or "good day".

2. Saying please and thank you: It's important to be polite when asking for something in Italy. To say "please", use the word "Per favore" (pronounced "pehr fa-voh-reh"). To say "thank you", use the phrase "Grazie" (pronounced "grah-tsee-eh").

3. Ordering food and drinks: When ordering food or drinks, it's helpful to know a few key phrases. "Un caffè" (pronounced "oon kah-fay") means "a coffee", while "Un

bicchiere di vino" (pronounced "oon bee-kee-eh-reh dee vee-noh") means "a glass of wine". To ask for the check, say "Il conto, per favore" (pronounced "eel kohn-toh pehr fa-voh-reh").

4. Tipping: Tipping is not as common in Italy as it is in other countries, but it's still appreciated for exceptional service. It's customary to leave a small amount of change, rather than a percentage of the bill. If you receive excellent service, you can leave a larger tip, but it's not expected.

5. Dress code: Italians tend to dress up more than people in other countries, especially when going out to dinner or to a nice event. Avoid wearing shorts or flip-flops to more formal places, and try to dress modestly when visiting churches or other religious sites.

6. Gestures: Italians are known for using hand gestures when they talk, and some of these gestures may seem confusing to non-Italians. For example, when Italians want to say "what do you want?", they'll raise their eyebrows and shrug their shoulders. If they want to say "I don't know", they'll make a circular motion with their hand.

7. Safety: Like any big city, Rome has its share of safety concerns. It's important to be aware of your surroundings and keep an eye on your belongings. Be cautious when using public transportation, especially at night. Avoid carrying large amounts of cash or expensive jewelry, and be wary of pickpockets in crowded tourist areas.

By familiarizing yourself with these common Italian phrases and customs, you'll be better equipped to enjoy your time in Rome and connect with the local culture.

here are some additional tips and phrases to help visitors navigate Italian culture:

- Tipping is not mandatory in Italy as a service charge is often included in the bill. However, it's common to leave some small change or round up the bill as a gesture of appreciation for good service.

- Italians tend to dress more formally than Americans, especially when going out to dinner or other social events. Dressing up a bit can show respect for the culture and help visitors blend in.

- When entering churches, it's important to dress modestly and cover the shoulders and knees out of respect for religious customs.

- Italians place a high value on family and social relationships. Greetings and small talk are important, and it's considered polite to ask how someone's day is going before jumping into business or other topics.

- Learning a few key Italian phrases can go a long way in showing respect for the culture and making connections with locals. Some useful phrases include:

- Buongiorno (Good morning)
- Buonasera (Good evening)
- Per favore (Please)
- Grazie (Thank you)
- Prego (You're welcome)
- Mi scusi (Excuse me/pardon me)
- Parla inglese? (Do you speak English?)
- Posso avere il conto, per favore? (May I have the bill, please?)

By keeping these tips in mind and making an effort to learn a few key Italian phrases, visitors can show respect for the local culture and make the most of their time in Rome.

Practical information on visas, health, and insurance for Rome travel

Visiting Rome can be an exciting and memorable experience, but it's important to make sure you have all the necessary practical information before your trip. Here is a detailed guide on practical information for visiting Rome:

1. **Visas:** If you're a citizen of a country within the European Union (EU), you don't need a visa to visit Rome or any other part of Italy. If you're a citizen of a country outside the EU, you may need a visa, depending on the length of your stay and the purpose of your trip. It's best to check with the Italian embassy or consulate in your country to determine if you need a visa and how to obtain one.

2. **Health:** Italy has a high standard of healthcare, but it's always wise to take

precautions to ensure a healthy and safe trip. Here are some tips:

- Make sure your routine vaccines are up-to-date
- Get travel insurance that covers emergency medical care
- Bring any necessary prescription medication, along with a copy of the prescription and a note from your doctor

3. **Insurance:** It's always a good idea to have travel insurance that covers emergencies and unforeseen circumstances such as lost luggage or flight cancellations. This can save you a lot of hassle and money in case of any problems.
4. **Safety:** Rome is a relatively safe city, but like any major city, it's important to take precautions to avoid any issues. Here are some safety tips:

- Keep your valuables safe, such as by using a money belt or keeping them in a secure location
- Be aware of pickpockets, especially in crowded tourist areas

- Avoid walking alone at night in quiet or poorly lit areas
- Use licensed taxis or public transportation to avoid scams

5. **Currency:** The official currency of Italy is the Euro (EUR). It's best to exchange your currency before you arrive in Rome, or withdraw Euros from an ATM once you arrive. Be aware that many shops and restaurants may not accept credit cards, so it's wise to carry cash.

6. **Language:** The official language of Italy is Italian, but many Romans speak English, especially in tourist areas. However, it's always helpful to learn some basic Italian phrases to communicate with locals and show your respect for their culture.

7. **Weather:** Rome has a Mediterranean climate, with mild winters and hot summers. It's best to visit in the spring or

fall when temperatures are milder and crowds are smaller. Be sure to pack appropriate clothing for the season, including comfortable walking shoes for exploring the city.

8. **Transportation:** Rome has an extensive public transportation system, including buses, trams, and a metro system. It's best to purchase a Roma Pass or other public transportation pass to save money and avoid the hassle of buying tickets individually. Taxis are also available, but they can be expensive, especially for longer distances.

In conclusion, visiting Rome can be an incredible experience, but it's important to have all the necessary practical information before your trip. By following these tips and guidelines, you can ensure a safe, enjoyable, and memorable trip to the Eternal City.

In addition to obtaining a visa and travel insurance, it's important to be aware of the health risks and precautions when visiting Rome. Italy is generally considered a safe country for travelers, but it's always wise to take basic safety precautions, such as keeping an eye on your belongings and being aware of your surroundings.

Here are some additional practical tips for your Rome travel:

1. **Currency:** Italy uses the Euro (EUR) as its currency. It's recommended to exchange some money before arriving in Rome, as exchange rates at airports and tourist areas can be unfavorable. There are also plenty of ATMs throughout the city where you can withdraw Euros.

2. **Electrical outlets:** Italy uses Type F electrical outlets, which are the same as the standard European two-pin plugs. It's a good idea to bring a universal adapter if you plan on using electronic devices.

3. **Tipping**: Tipping in Rome is not as common as in the United States, but it is still appreciated in some circumstances. In restaurants, a service charge is typically included in the bill, but it's common to leave a small tip for exceptional service. For other services, such as taxis or hairdressers, it's customary to round up the bill or leave a small tip.

4. **Public transportation**: Rome has an extensive public transportation system, including buses, trams, and the metro. A single ticket costs €1.50 and is valid for 100 minutes of travel on any combination of buses, trams, or metro lines. It's also possible to purchase a day pass or multi-day pass, which can be more cost-effective for longer stays.

5. **Weather:** Rome has a Mediterranean climate, with hot summers and mild winters. The peak tourist season is from May to September, when temperatures can

be quite high. It's a good idea to pack sunscreen, a hat, and lightweight clothing if you're visiting during the summer months.

By following these practical tips, you can make your trip to Rome safe and enjoyable. Remember to be respectful of the local culture and customs, and don't be afraid to ask for help or advice if you need it. Happy travels!

Printed in Great Britain
by Amazon